AFTER TED & SYLVIA

After Ted
& Sylvia

Crystal Hurdle

RONSDALE PRESS

AFTER TED & SYLVIA
Copyright © 2003 Crystal Hurdle

RONSDALE PRESS
3350 West 21st Avenue
Vancouver, B.C., Canada
V6S 1G7

Edited by Ronald B. Hatch
Typesetting: Julie Cochrane, in New Baskerville 11 pt on 13.5
Cover Design: Rand Berthaudin, Pause Communications
Author Photo: Scott Braley
Paper: Ancient Forest Friendly Rolland "Enviro" — 100% post-consumer
    waste, totally chlorine-free and acid-free

Ronsdale Press wishes to thank the Canada Council for the Arts, the Government of Canada through the Book Publishing Industry Development Program (BPIDP), and the Province of British Columbia through the British Columbia Arts Council for their support of its publishing program.

National Library of Canada Cataloguing in Publication Data

Hurdle, Crystal, 1958–
    After Ted & Sylvia / Crystal Hurdle.

    Poems.
    ISBN 1-55380-010-9

    1. Hughes, Ted, 1930 — Poetry. 2. Plath, Sylvia — Poetry. I. Title. II. Title: After Ted and Sylvia.
PS8565.U73A82 2003   C811'.6   C2003-910699-3
PR9199.4.H865A82 2003

At Ronsdale Press we are committed to protecting the environment. To this end we are working with Markets Initiative (www.oldgrowthfree.com) and printers to phase out our use of paper produced from ancient forests. This book is one step towards that goal.

Printed in Canada by AGMV Marquis

CONTENTS

for Scott in this life

for Sylvia and Ted in the next

ACKNOWLEDGEMENTS

This book, while based on the lives of poets Sylvia Plath and Ted Hughes, is a work of the imagination. It attempts to unravel their intertwined lives by adopting and speaking in the several voices of people involved. It is hoped that many will be inspired to read poetry by Plath and Hughes: that the already converted will revisit their work and that others might be prompted to explore it.

I wish to offer thanks to my Capilano College English students, particularly those inspiring souls in English 209 and Creative Writing classes; to the participants of the Sylvia Plath Symposium at the University of Indiana, in fall 2002, for their positive reception of these poems; to the members of Stretchers for their fabulous suggestions, wit and encouragement; and to Bill Schermbrucker, unpaid editor, mentor, friend.

Versions of these poems have appeared in or have been accepted for publication in *Canadian Literature, Whetstone, Event, The Prairie Journal of Canadian Literature, The Windsor Review, The Capilano Review, The Dalhousie Review,* and *Grain.*

Quotations in "Laureate V" are from *The Secret Language of Birthdays,* by Gary Goldschneider and Joost Eiffers.

The BC Health Guide is referred to in "Sivvy: Review."

The chemistry problem in "Sivvy: Furlough in the Periodic Table" is adapted from Charles E. Mortimer's *Chemistry: A Conceptual Approach.*

"Sivvy: Panic, My Alcatraz" contains quotations from "Rock of Ages," by Joan Didion.

LAUREATE

Laureate I: Blooms

for Susan

The drooping boutonnieres
of two dead wives
wear him.

He cannot help
inhaling their musky scents
redolent after decades.

They can still
deepen the timbre of his voice
marionette his gentled lamb's hands
into swooping grace
leech his blood into passion's ink.

They beseech him out of passive grief
to bear
daffodil bouquets for Assia
rose gardens for Sylvia.

Laureate II: Paper Dolls

Actor acted upon,
a character in the fiction
of his living.

He is flattened onto the backs
of drafts of his own old poems and hers.
Critics cut with pruning shears,
manicure scissors.

Folding creates hand-held
images of himself, similar.

Here a rapid rip gives
him clawed hands.
Here the craggy nose is
beaklike, predatory.
Here the shock of hair is
frankly seductive.

The blackened silhouette
of a grieving man
shadows the papers.

Her Heptonstall grave
has become a metal mine.
Scissors smile.

Laureate III: To You, Dear Ted

for Bill

after reading Ted Hughes' *Birthday Letters*

You're right about us, Ted.
We amateur literary critics
instructors at second-rate institutions
have used Sylvia as a bright lure
for other junior enquiring minds
(who write "Slyvia")
seeking scurrilous death poetry
scandal, a love affair
gone rotten from within
an apple, wormy, shrivelled.
You wouldn't know that once
we had imagined
erudite wit, polished cunning
in our classrooms
in our fusty offices
vacuumed twice a year
to remove the shells
of peanuts and almonds
of mildewed coronets from leftover candy floss
our fingers' debris.

It's been easy to slip into Sylvia's shoes
— though all of us at once
makes a shriekingly tight fit —
to experience her torments
her manic exultations.

On the top-heavy side, her confessions
her lugubrious journals
her poetic Morse code messages
from the cave of her foetid hair.
And now, another side
your lyric tribute
your puzzlement
your helium in her long unused
collapsed symbols
— red, elm, moon, bell jar, heart, yews —
your own air that distorts voice
in those bright balloons
so full that they are lovely, lovely
a springtime beckoning
and we hunger
we are sated
speak in tongues
until, so turgid
they burst.

These rubbery bits will not decompose, Ted,
will poppy petal your twinned graves, Ted,
because your plot is waiting
because the story is not over
until we say it's over. Ted.

Maybe the fat lady has sung
or not.
The lady reduced to lithe fish.

Your pain?
Aurelia conveniently dead?
The time ripe as Sylvia's burgeoning daffodils?
Money required for a trip abroad?
Back to Spain with someone who likes it?
Funding required for new foundations
for Sylvia's Devon house now
sinking in the heavy English mud?

Yes, Ted, it's your side
and a sweet side it is
Your manly, musky grief
Your desire for privacy
(Or, as you English say, "pri-ivacy,"
like privy
full of stool and euphemism)
Yourself, impermeable, impenetrable wall.

Anne couldn't get on the estate,
never mind near the wall,
as you and Olwyn bricked a new fortress
around her, her very own mortared bell jar.
Janet climbed your wall with lifted skirts
for easy movement.

Against those forward distaff flanks
those rappelling females
drawbridges faltered over moats
and raised creakily over beseeching hands.

Through it all
you mocked from above
created origami snow with
smiling scissors
the worst blizzard England had seen
played with the cauldron
of molten oil
saw how far it would tip
before spilling over
polished your workboots to crush
greedy, groping fingers.

Still, with enough fingers
laid end to end
to circle the world twice
we have to say
some of the poems are lovely, Ted
could make us weep, Ted
almost left us breathless
but enquiring minds want more
than puzzlement and grief
admission of love and loss
a bell jar distortion.

We hear your howling wolves
see your cocooned babes
but we don't hear your bongo drums
smell your boozy laughter
after the funeral.
We can read her one novel
but not her other, lost, oh so lost.

We, in Canada, even worse than in "your" America,
had the Dionne quints on show
for years, in charming cages
admission a small coinage.
What about wifey #3?
What about dead Assia and her dead baby?
What about Frieda and Nicholas?

Suffer the little children.
The peanut-crunching crowd
wants more than gnawed bones
derivative sop. More flesh. More blood.

Ted, you beguile us with the second person
— you you you you you —
not always Sylvia,
but we lovelorn female
readers, writers, critics,
too academic for Harlequins,
we resent your You's.

You blame her female mentors,
her uncanny darkness.
You blame her Mummy and her Daddy,
calling, calling her into the abyss.
But you don't blame yourself.

What a P.R. job you've done.
Poet Laureate, grieving husband,
dearest father, charmster executor.
But enough already, back to your plots,
lie, lie.

Ted, you should have waited
had these poems published posthumously
as you published her work (what you had not lost).
But as always there's calculation
in your craft.
Without breaking the threads
held in your cunning fingers
you control and spin the myth
pretty, ephemeral candy floss
as you manipulate the marionette strings.

What is it about you, Ted?
A cunning bedside manner?
A politician's use of words?
Or is it this measured, pretty puzzlement?

Bewilderment is not sweet
in an old old man.

Bring on more women
for your incandescent flame.
All the You's, Hughes, in the direct address.
Burning pyres for birthday letters.

Of course, this is not the whole story.
It never is
though we want it.
We have waited thirty-five years
for these letters,
a lifetime, a lifeline.
We've ripped through instalment one.
Instalment two, please,
and be quick about it, Ted.
Our numbers are legion, Ted.
We peanut crunchers have lips
wider and more rubbery than Sylvia's
a gaggle of tombstone teeth
and raging, enraged appetites.

Laureate IV: Obituary

for Ted Hughes

I)

A murder of crows.
Who murdered whom?
Crow flies into a dark hole, whole.
He is not at peace.

A murder of crows unites
but one, a straggler
and the V elongates
like the spread of their wings as
they fly and fly.

Wolves slink and drag their tails
in a cacophony, a chorus of howls.

The clock ticks.
Outside, no star shines.
And the thought-fox screams its abandonment
as it circles
three-legged and bloody
in the snow.

Crow is bewildered. He is more alone than ever.

II)

Its era was over.
The literary loves
a poetic fiction.

Your cast of characters mostly dead.
The crone mother barely there
ill and in a nursing home.
Long quietened: the father's
guttural plosives
base and melancholy
all those voices ululating, beseeching
your wife from the dark side
to the dark side.
Hers too.

And now you too cross over.

   III)

In heaven,
two moons eclipse each other
and blacken velvet skies.
The hawk alights on the elm tree.

The bride and groom lie
hidden for three days.
After that, resurrection
understood even by pagans.

Bell jar lifts
and becomes sanctuary.
Fox is a living
wedding veil.

Votives: bouquets of meadow grass,
burnished maples,
and a single out-of-season
daffodil.

IV)

The death hand flat-palmed
like a traffic cop's
forces reverence.
It flattens out wrinkles
in the fabric of loss and grief.
The hush of silks
beneath the photos
draped in garland and ribbons.
The head shot as craggy
as the landscape
you are now part of.

You are no longer a bastard
but a loving, private man
vindicated by your own death.

How differently we read things
through the blood-stained eyes
of recent, unexpected loss.
Death ameliorates.

But enough:
manufacturing grief
like consent
is a sorry business.

V)

Her Scorpio birth.
Your Scorpio death.
Stubborn, willful, you
hung on for an extra day.
No satisfaction in making her
a birthday present of your death.
Birthday Letters was enough.

Hers the Day of Impulse.
Yours the Day of Explosive Power.
Characteristics "a strong desire to protect
private life" and "forbidding enough
to keep admirers at arm's length."

She died on the Day of Improved Comfort:
"The pursuit of pleasure ultimately
involves the suffering of pain."

You died on the Day of Research:
"Learning when to let go
and allow things to happen
on their own is
indeed a practiced art."

Birthday Letters is back
to number one.
Come back, Ted.
Rebirth Letters?
The window is starless still.
Imagine
something
else
is
alive

VI)

The flag is
at half-mast.
Poetry unbound.

Who will write for you
as you did for them?

Not the Royals
Not Mummy and Daddy
Not your bewildered bewildering Sylvia.

What hubris appropriating
another's life, another's grief
for poetic fodder.

Opportunistic. Carrion Crow.
You will never die again.

VII)
The blood jet is poetry.
So, too, rivulets of tears,
creek beds, freshets, rivers.
River for you, Ted.

River. River. River.

I think of October salmon,
of fish eggs, eels, steelhead trout
I think of the siren call of the river
your river, life, a new life.

Cry me a river. I cry a river.

VIII)
No longer the toddler
of the grainy photos
Frieda feeds the fire
a torch-bearing poet.

Nicholas tills the soil,
rich with humus.
A lover of the land
like you.

Both your gravestones are unsettled
in the harsh, autumnal earth.
The wind buffets their scarred inscriptions.

Inside, it is almost warm.
With weary fondness, Carol watches
as Frieda's Laszlo
rolls a paintbrush
between index finger and thumb,
snakes green, hums green,
through your Devon study
no longer brown.

Frieda's disquieting painting
on your dust jacket,
green, blue, red, red, red,
burns with fierce flame.

Laureate V: Poem for Sylvia

The Task: to pin you down, dear Sylvia
like one of Nabokov's butterflies
beautiful specimen
though you still struggle

I'm on your trail
Chalk Farm
Primrose Hill
The winding streets
warmer warmer
now I'm in your neighborhood
yours and Ted's

And why can't I write
a poem without you, Ted?
Dear Ted. Dead Ted.

No yew tree in sight
Chalcott Square
now being gentrified
Your third floor flat gutted
Hardly a sniff of you in the renovation
lilac lavender
all white inside
faintly glowing
the inside a jewel
opal onyx
or something even purer
A mother wheels her stroller by.
No unwieldy prams now.

How about a fine detail?
rolled toweling against the kitchen door
to keep the gas in
but didn't you
who wrote sestinas and villanelles
during the delightful explosions
of the chemistry lectures
you faked your way through
know that gas rises?
Good Lord! What of
the sweet babes
a floor above?

Around the corner
123 Fitzroy Road
Blue plaqued for Yeats
but not for you.
You only wrote most of *Ariel* here
you only died here
Soot-drab beleaguered
you have been removed from your own life
No wolves howl
A solitary bird caws
Mellow workaday thrum

Later, bookstore in Charing Cross
a bio of you

I had been at the wrong address
Number 3 not 7 Chalcott square
Your real place was at the corner of my eye
a floater on the
periphery of my vision
just almost there

like "Mountain" not "Fountain" in *Pale Fire*

a placebo effect
dead ends
cul-de-sacs
false starts and mistaken leads
and I a poor detective
You are hard to pin down even in death

And what about Ted
writing as unwitting bystander
at an accident?
"Her husband" he calls himself
Editor of your work
he slips cagily between the bounds
of first person and third
in your introductions, his forewords
but I want the boldness of second person.
Hey, YOU! YOU rancorous bastard.

And what about the passive voice
her marriage novel that "disappeared"
as did she?
It was her or me,
you said. One of us had to die.

Strings of women
from Aurelia to Lady Lazarus
to Assia to Carol and many more.
The fecundity of laureate-ship.
Ted, will you stay out of this poem?
For Christ's sake!
It's for Sylvia.
Her ghost in the hard drive.
She will not be subsumed.

Try again.
Catalogue the most striking images:
daffodils, red, the milk and the rusks
the rising gas(those sweet babes!)
the bitch of a mother
the Nazi daddy
the virile husband who replaced him.

Get lost, Ted. Go fuck yourself
instead of someone else.

The theories:
a set of fairy tales
with bad endings out of the Brothers Grimm
manic depressive or bad PMS?
Suicide is not creative.

How about some naproxen
prozac on your grave?
I'll ping the pills off
your lotus tombstone
how about some happy poems
those who read you must not fall in love
with your easeful death
but the you of your work
you yew

Voyeur I am
weeping with frustration now
it's too big
there's way too much for this poem
those burning letters
those pathetic homes
the theories
the sister-in-law
the orphans
the pellucid poetry
the poetry the poetry

It is too hard I am tired so tired
but I will hunt you
through the neat paw print phonemes
of your poems.
Out of your blackness
I will drag you by your hair
so that you might live
into the sun into the fucking sun
so sue me
you self-righteous, too clever by half, wearying
Ted was right
bitch

Laureate VI: Wife

I)

On whose behalf are you here?

the dreariness of North Tawton
inbreeding
grizzled
monosyllabic
inhabitants
Who could stand it?

owl beaked
a cross between a crow and a fox
but not creature of his imagining
implacable
Carol

It is my house now
Lady of the Manor
like the Arundels of years ago
No blue plaque here
but he's been dead only two years

I was married to him for 28 years
the claim the dispatch the stake
Please respect my wishes
weary weary

these hordes of women
followers
seekers

II)

He takes refuge
in ordinariness.

After a psychotic poet genius
and a Russian silken seductress
this nurse
hempen homespun
he brings her to this house
of other women, other wives
thatch roofed like a cock-eyed hat
on this Bluebeard's castle
but there is no locked room
and his rangy body is no key

All the rooms are open
the soft footfalls of the dead women
every day

near, the yew tree grows bigger
not succumbing to root rot, to aphids' honeydew
to her fierce spade
She scores its roots deeply
when she upturns Assia's tulips,
Sylvia's daffodil bulbs
and tamps in her own impatiens
they wither in the yew's ballooning shade
the rag rug gyrates and squirms from her grasp
not for it the dustbin
the Aga has years of life left in it
longer than the years of the two dead wives

it is easy to become worn out

eyebrows in the eaves
lashes in the drains

it is too open
he pretends to be so

they are in his past
she is his future

but how can this be
when the very walls mock her with Sylvia's redness
that a paintbrush has not yet been made
to obscure.
They glow even through the new wallpapers
the doorways constrict with their soft ghostly hips
as she tries to squeeze through

     It's my house now

if she says it often enough,
she will believe it

     On whose behalf have you come?
Sylvia's? Assia's? any other woman's?

She trips over breasts on the thresholds
coiling thighs lolling tongues
How much easier it would be if
there were
only one room to stay out of

Ted writes in his corner room
It is his
has always been
What has been his is now hers
so she must share the wives
They smile and smile, crimson lipped
melt in the walls
the thatch gripping their hair

III)

On whose behalf are you here?

my own, strictly my own
Is this the house of Lord and Lady Arundel?

Yes, but it's my house now.
[repeat repeat]

The yew needles are singing
with new voice
with new story . . .

IV)

I am sick of them
the sharing
the secretiveness
the women before and after
Ted's infidelities, legion.

A man must have his meat.
No easy succor for me in suicide.

I am of the earth.

I am sick of
his two dead wives
who will always exist
his book about her
he had been writing for years
and I never knew any of it
pining, all of us pining
she is still a wraith in my house
How can I wrest it from these women?
The biographers, the feminist slags,
always Sylvia, always Assia
always after him
my beloved
even even
and in his final months
bone thin, becoming a wraith
he spent weekends, weeks
away from Court Green with one more
always another

I've painted over the hearts
foolish totems
but even the wind of the yew tree breathes her
and today
another one at the end of my lane
leggy, knapsacked — a quester

On whose behalf are you here?

ghosts in the house
in the nearby churchyard
some rising for over 200 years
their old gravestones defend my privacy
but the two-year death is the hardest
He is not here
and I have outlived them all.

V)

He never wrote about me.
about Assia occasionally
about Sylvia in brooding bursts
a bookful after thirty-five years
longer than she was alive
but not for me

It is a mark of honour, respect
surely

not of my steadfastness
my nurturing
my husband, my seeming child
my blanket of humility and good grace

his fiercest defender against those ravening women
the critics
the feminists
even the lovers
I always found them out
sought them out

I am sick of muse men
this time, pray, not a poet
not a womanizer
someone who will love me for my own self

he did not write about me
unless I am of the Moortown landscape
Orchards he cultivated along with my father
the spark of his children's verse
but not of my polished eyes
my sleek frame
my burnished hair
the colour of freshly tilled earth beneath

he did not write about me

our coffee mornings
the slant of the sunlight through
the second-best bedroom window
He did not write about me
I am out of the public eye
he did not

VI)

The Seeker wonders,
Why is the lady walking towards me?
I am almost at Sylvia and Ted's house.
My camera is ready.
Did she forget something?
She seems to want to talk to me.
She is dressing me down.
She is the lady of the house.

Why am I here?
            On whose behalf have you come?

On your behalf. On yours.
Ted's widow.
To meet a minor character in a seedy
but loved story
though her own life
I will write it read it
savour the slow flip of the leaves
notice her small presence
in the dusky dark corners
and sweep her out

SEEK

The Poetry Class Reconvenes

Ted,
your photographs
I circulate
in glassine envelopes
for protection

Tactile psychology of disgust
Too British
Huge bald spot
Greasy hair
No comment
He looks like a pedophile

To those who haven't breathed you
it's hard
to explain
your charisma
In two dimensions, dissipated
your energy mere oil slick

but in life
you were larger than
life

Milk: Apocrypha

For Sylvia, the night is veiled and noxious
The moon is scant
Bathtub full of seepage, pipes frozen
Inside and out it hurts to breathe
London is not supposed to be so cold

Alone, excepting the children,
as on Christmas Eve,
but it is almost Valentine's
and Sylvia without her husband muse
He is in Devon with that woman
her name a hot hiss

The basket chair leaves welts
She drifts into the kitchen
worries a mug of lemon tea for the flu
A new poem? No?
Too late, Better in the morning
She writes her letters
and pounds the stamps askew
with her fists

Adult resignation
to believe fairy tales
are for children
Innocence lasts only so long

Treats for the visiting one
or for the one who is left?
Her proffering:
Two mugs of milk and rusks of bread
before the cribs
before the last descent
before the gas.

Did she think
Nicholas would glug eagerly from his cup
would not howl for her absent breast?
And what of Frieda, the barely big sister?
Did she think?
How could she?

Not the mistress usurper but
the good mother becomes the wicked queen
moon goddess who kills the good mother
and leaves them

one floor above
bodies sluggish from the rising gas
starfished in their cribs
tipping over those mugs of milk
in the early vacant morning
crying for their mother

Fervent 103°

Sylvia,
never mind my
maternal instinct nil
husband not a strong dark poet god
oven electric instead of gas

I want

your blackly comic invective
to rappel from my page
not dribbling
as from frozen pipes in a raw London

your mushrooms' coyness
their macabre power in meekness
their bell-jar curvature

babies' laughter voluptuous roses
tulips with teeth
the draughty phases of the moon

all the facets of your drawn face
mournful and vengeful daughter/wife
catty genius and bitch goddess

your words, knives
slicing cleanly
severing to the bone

your eerie tone
sleight of hand that even now makes
syllabic pellets unfurl into flame

to become conflagration

I want I want I want

Digging for You,

Sylvia

Shards of broken lives
With them
we will comb
the Devon fields
and the pig farms in Coquitlam
with the toothbrushes
you said you couldn't put in your poems
map off every square centimetre
so we won't miss an iota
a sniff, a breath
a single speck of DNA
even one of your tawny hairs
the hot salt of your last-day tears

Robert William Pickton indicted on how many counts?
With all those shards
we can sink him into the black Devon dirt
or your wet Yorkshire grave
We will bring back the women
all the murdered women

Build a bonfire and resurrect them
They will stream out of the earth
hot lava
pure elemental dangerous
And you will lead them
What pretty faces!
What gorgeous hair!

The Sylvias: a Fantasy

I

Salacious tempting Sylvias.
Seductresses at seven.
Daddy's little girls,
a pair of Colossus Electra lovers.

II

Exorcise the Daddies.
Both are evil Nazis.
One cement-toed.
The other hook-handed.
One cleft-chinned.
The other blood-bespattered.

Suffer the little children
unto them.
Suffocate small daughters with
fellatio turnabout.
Curled blondies both.

III

Pretty little Sylvias.
How does your Daddy grow?
With slug bait
and snake-rat tails
and besmirched daughters all in a row.

IV

Prim-lipped mother Aurelia or Adelaide.
Entreaties of disapproval.
Lips puckered,
not for a kiss,
lemon sour
pickle pussed.

Pandora's monkeys
see no evil
hear no evil
speak no evil.
Pandora's fiddlers three.

Esther's three disquieting muses.
Esther's three times
three times to die.
Esther's pseudonyms
Electra, Elaine, Sylvia.

Holy triumvirates.

V

Daddy keeps bees.
She licks the
pollen off his fingers
Sepal-honeyed.

Other Daddy, like the Breadman,
Offers chocolate cookies and cherry tarts.
Pluck a cherry for a cherry.
Daddy sucks on her
Chiclet teeth from the Candy Factory.

Q. Why is semen white and
urine yellow?
A. So a Daddy can tell if
he's coming or going.
The little Sylvias laugh,
choke on hot salt,
gag on Daddysperm.

VI

Adelaide washes the
family's linen in
the bowels of a Daddy's house in
the basement wringer washer.
She sweats tears
makes the stains flatten
whiskerwhisper thin as drawn lips.
Bleached with sanctimoniousness.
Not everything goes on the
backyard line.

VII

Daddy. Daddy.
Lysol for the germs.
She likes it.
Big. Bigger. Biggest.

VIII

Featureless
(like a fine Jew linen)
other selves,
the sexually responsive
little girls,
phallic-headed as the disquieting muses,
who
can't remember
can't remember
can't remember

Except.

Esther has to get back to her daddy,
to pay her daddy back.
Equivocal Hate.
Amphibolous Love.

Dying to lose
her virginity,
she's lost it already.
Daddy. Daddy.
Mustn't tell. Mustn't mustn't.

After the sophomore prom,
Sylvia's date cups
one breast, and she cries.

Accept.

Hush hush hush.

IX

The silence breeds
gifts for poetry, for prose
engorged with rage.
The viscous musty wetness
of fatherly love.
The resolution to
eat men.

X

Aurelia lays out
the picnic on the sands.
The Sylvias watch from
Daddy's ears,
orifices as yet untried.

Adelaide calls and calls for
her little girl.
Nobody comes but Daddy.

The Sylvias penetrate the ears.
Twin Aphrodites
daddy-erected from the gargoyle head.

XI

Daddy begotten.
Daddy betrayed.
Daddy behold.
Daddy be dead.

    (not yet. not yet.)

XII

Breast-shaped as Otto's hives,
the bell jar distorts.
Talons scrape and bleed on
reflection.
The specimens, goggle-
eyed,
careen against
the convex walls.
A pair of golden bugs shiny

caught
caught
caught.

      (yet. yet.)

XIII

Daddy's little girls
are no more.
The damned Daddy is dead.

The bell jar fissures.
Two wan women
stagger out
and squinttwist their vacant eyes
against the brilliant sun.

Names

Spell check won't recognize your name
it puzzles and puzzles
straggly red underlining
pontifical: do you mean *"plash"*?

You exist in homophones
you who so loved your thesaurus
better than any bible

your surname, like *platy*
a variation of the family *Poeciliidae*
duck-billed = rubbery lipped?
Sylvia *Platypus*?

or used chiefly of mineral formations
or with Low German, *Plattdeutsch,*
ach, du

plat, a small patch of land
where you now lie
plotted, plotting

plate, domestic hollowware
marriage filleted you, deboned you

or given as a prize
to the winner in a contest
but whose?

the theory of tectonics
for you the earth moved
measuring what on the Richter scale?

Made more valuable by your first name
not quite gold
but almost as good as
Mummy's sweet, *silvery* Sivvy

frequenting groves and woods
you sought it as pseudonym
Sylvan, a perfectly euphonious magazine name
asexual
asylvia

salvia, your two-lipped open calyx and red flowers
for all the world to see
as your daddy wanted

choosing amongst your many *selves*
who will not recognize you?

Primary Colours

painters try to slow down
your perception, make you stare
at a painting until you've absorbed

it but who wants to slow down to see
through luminescent pores
to become the blue of *Spirit of Fire*
a stamen's honey in *The Tangled Garden*
a blur in a Monet lily
the yellow of a Van Gogh sunflower
bright blanket to crawl
into and under away from
the winter rains

death or rebirth by landscape
to become one with the picture
disappearing, emerging, two-dimensional,
trapped, trapezoid, the spot of the i
at the gyre's tip

to become a pointillist dot,
or the dot of one of the 300
"i"s in the 300 "rhinos,"
colourful collage,
red yellow blue,
in the shape of a rhino's
tumescent horn
rhinorhinorhinorhinorhino
ever diminishing
the space at the funnel's nadir,
beginning and end of the echo of
Munch's silent scream

or in Klee's *Anxiety*
to become one with the eye of
the fish staring you down and in into

wove paper weaving words
to become the long vowels
an oblique in a disquieting diphthong
of Plath's painting poetry
from lost, lost, only to be

found in De Chirico's
darning-headed muses
Plath's disturbing inspirations
who say slow down and stare at us
absorb us become one with us

in Rousseau's *The Dream,*
Yadwigha on her red couch,
in Sylvia too, gesturing, commanding
closer, closer, a detail from
her left nipple
a pore of the areola
vibrant, bitter red

the lure and threat of art's red

red, read, ready for
the frisson in watching
the performance poet create *Red*

red red red

in the words from his mouth "Red"
"carmine, violet, violent valentine red"
from his fingers
on his face.
His teeth are red.
His shoulders are red.
His eyelids are red.
Red paint beneath him behind him.
When the ceiling opens
the sky is aflame with red.

Carmine in the blood.
Absorption. Red. Read.

SIGHT

Teacher of Sylvia

about someone who taught Sylvia
or a teacher who looks
at her work?
What is object
what is subject?
Consider the tense
Is there an object lesson here?

Signup sheet's on my door
for oral reports
and they go for Plath

(Crystal, is that metonymy or synecdoche?
What was that "a" word?
Is there an am-am-amphiboly?)

always a plaintive curiosity
that erodes my heart

(is *that* metonymy or synecdoche?)
pencils worn slant
lips blued by ink

Sylvia, just keeping you posted
You're still
intoxicating
after all these years
the Marilyn Monroe of poetry
your lipsticked smile
your shroud raised
like her red dress
a peek-a-boo banner
your piquant perfume of despair

they all want that whiff
of the grave
that old death-distracting soft shoe
one, two
one, two
and you
and you

(epistrophe *and* anaphora?
or vice-versa?)
the clutch of the laundry list

(I never could keep those straight)

nor you

(I am always remembering
what I am trying to forget)

nor you
and you
not you

Ground Cover

Sylvia,
away from the landscape of home,
you took umbrage at the hawthorn
its black ether
duplicitous spines

Here we have salal, salmon berries
cedars like Cambridge's spires
dark firs piercing the sky

and skunk cabbages:

in spring
forests' candles
phallic, reverent
A yellow more captivating
than daffodils'

but with the anaesthetizing stink
of your cadaver room

Seeker on Mountains

Don't get angry with me now, Sivvy
You don't have to be the whirling dervish
with the lime-green eyes
citric, septic
Please let me address your sweet complicit side

you who loved the rich fall days at Smith
when a dean declared, "Mountain Day!"
All classes were cancelled
for hikes in the red-leaved hills
your page boy bobbing with your laughter

you who loved being mountainous pregnant
with your husband
reveling in the bigness of your belly
birthing poems and babies both

I saw Ted at sixty
and he was a tor of a man
my knees weak
as when cycling up a steep incline
too absorbed for the mesmerizing view
His words were emerald boulders
hailing
It was all I could do
to weave crazily among
them
to
his

                          peak

with him, every day
an unhoped for blessing?
with him, every day
a Mountain Day?

A Sivvy Sighting on the Picket line

Labor unrest
transit strike
clogs on your feet
and in the streets
you blister

in your high nasal twang
earnestly, you argue
over the picket line that
they enjoy good wages that
you had to make things up
out of whole cloth! that
their working hours are regular that
your flat was always smaller
than your hopes! that
their daily task requires
little thought
and even less ambition that
hoping for pittances of cash
you wrote and you wrote and you wrote!

stuck-up smarmy bitch, the workers grunt
with their dented thermoses
and hard, heavy sandwich boards

Driving ain't about poetry but
Roses are red
Violets are blue
We sure all would
like to fuck you

Barbie and Ken

Barbie as Elizabeth Taylor
see those fetching eyebrows
Barbie as Judy Garland as Dorothy
note the ruby red slippers
Barbie as Morticia
find her widow's peak

and another special edition Barbie
Barbie as you
clothes horse

a skirt, green dirndl
with tiny black, white, and electric-blue
shapes swarming across it

a Jaeger black and heavenly blue
tweed suit
and a metallic blue-and-black
French top
from Dickens & Jones

These and so many more choices
clothes to hurl off the roofs of buildings
matching white Samsonite luggage
thirty jumpers at one fell swoop

clothing as armor, thin protection
a pink wool suit to be married in
but what to be buried in?

and here's your Ken
in his plain black clothes
not many accessories for Ken
This Ken's needs are simple
More Barbies
Or more Barbie lookalikes

He moves with the women
into their play stations

Grow your hair, Barbie!
Become a writer, Barbie!
Gas yourself, Barbie!

See the play kitchen with everything you will need

The Other

much maligned
you with the pretty face
Assia
and the big hips
made for child bearing

and then only the one

and you, broken
as if his child's hand
encrusted with frost, pink-mittened
were playing rock paper scissors
with your heart

Block

Sivvy, I need Ted
to set me
free

or exercises
to massage me
out of writer's block

acres of painful tendons
between head and willing hand
numbness
no spark

What?
a moon? hemlock?
a willing cup
a sup
and then to join you?

Why, jealousy is not becoming
in you
or are you flattering me?
a friend in need
indeed?
A toast?

I've finished your book
Now I have given
us all up

as if for dead

Crystal Bubbles

for Jane Langton

A crystal ball recedes
witch woman seer poet
her cape her river of
acrid Scamander hair
all the better to frighten
little children with
in letters home

In the ball, a thin woman
beseechment in black and white
calls for her
and then the face of the other
starched pinafore screams

But you banished your Mummy
the ball, opaque,
became cosmic soap bubble
wafting wafting
The blue birds black and white

In my back yard
I squat
dip your snake charmer mouth-pipe
into the glistening foam
release a Gulf Stream of bubbles
you, all of you
you braided in a nurse's uniform
you skipping in a swimsuit

The bubbles bigger as you get older
but your face always your face
the convex images converge
a teaching wife
horse-loving poet
Death's new bride
An ill wind could blow them all away
fragile in the slip stream
of my imagination

Dropping your pipe of clay
shattering
watching my nails
with tender fists unfurling
I juggle so many Sylvias
a Sylvia for every age and mood and role
I make my cheeks chipmunk
and blow
hundreds thousands infinitesimal
into this world
and the next

Fetish

coiled neatness in envelopes
cunning
carefully scripted
Sylvia's hair at eight months
delicate, disturbing sweetness
not the animal whiff of Alvarez fame
horse mane
raw and unnerving

the delicacy of hair jewelry
a fine conceit
memorabilia of the dead
but no amber here to encase it
in envelopes almost translucent
from soft strokings
hands other than mine
precious paper
so easily rent
as you

long before you thought yourself
Jew victim
the hanks of hair
arranged, alphabetized
not many fetish objects here
your typewriter at Smith College
but you are my fetish
you you

Defiant
I slide one long hair
from an envelope
it's the color of a hazelnut
or your favorite coffee with cream
I could swallow it whole
you could be inside me

my fetish, my fetish

in the photo of you that is not here
your face bronze
a pale bikini
You are an Aztec goddess
worshipping the sun
your hair is tawny
you are your own muse

Ted grabbed your headband
red? blue?
on that first meeting
Some of your long hair snagged in that?
your Veronica Lake bangs?
Did he save those hairs
will of the wisp?
a hair-tidy of you amongst his pots
in the shed?
Ted not the conscientious documentary maker
that your mother was
For him,
a trophy
not a vital part of you

in braided coils like a princess crown
mixed with his greasy forelock on your shared pillow

I would have loved you better

"Apprehensions" as opera
It disturbs
The high notes might break glass
I wince with "wince"
It thrills
I write as if your eye
is upon me
My poem too will be operatic
I will practice singing
for you, Sylvia, anything
building a bridge to you through the clear notes
of Frieda's open mouth
through the decks of the tarot
through strong chains of your own hair
which I will thinly braid
coil around my own neck and hand
gag myself with
pulling as on a bridle
making the good Ariel lead
and coming on home to you

All I ask is a single hair

I will make a weaving of you
for you
the crowning thread in the almost middle
like a natural part
a weft shot of your golden hair

It will be secret between us two
I will stroke it
for a bubble of horrible joy

Fetish sounds like luscious,
or vicious, lascivious

Perverts maintain their fetishes lifelong
It's time to come out of that closet

In the creased envelope
I've left a thin moon
of my left index fingernail
freshly bitten for you

I know how to communicate
with the dead

The Psychiatrist's Diagnosis

my patient Crystal
you are identifying too much
with Sylvia Plath
You should learn to hate
your Mother, your Father
Yours is a sickness
sullen with narcissism

I helped Sylvia
Let me doctor you

As a nun and psychiatrist
I know both the psychical
and the spiritual worlds
the liminality between them
where I live
I know many needs

Sylvia worshipped me then
loves me now

I analyze and pray
with that dear one daily
Her knuckles are chilblained with prayer
She wishes for your sanity

In this profession
in order to succeed
one has to become ruthless
You are too needy

You are shivering
It is chill and not yet February
and without the virulence
of that wretched London winter
It is cold on your temples
when I apply the gel

My finger on the Record button
our sessions immortalized
in a river of audio-tape
Depending on the season
enough to skate across
cutting elegant figures
or to drown in
The voltage
will be cheaper than natural gas
the costs rising, pitiful, pathetic
so punishing
so warming
such a curative

SPEAK: SIVVY SEEKS TED;
OTHERS SEEK SYLVIA

—

Sivvy: Leaves

I read down here
in Purgatory
not much else to do
My pens are dried out
What I would give for my old Donne
that paperback Yeats with the effeminate face
your Shakespeare I made confetti of
anything dog-eared with fond remembrance

Book offerings have been meagre
top ten lists
what enquiring minds want to know
Inconsequentials the wraiths have pocketed
when stunned
they plummet into their journeys

But now, *Birthday Letters*
Apparently we're a best-seller

How dare you, dear
Dare
Dare

I shred and stitch laureate leaves
To the victor go the spoils

The Mother Speaks

I loved you before I met you.
I wanted only the best for you.
You always were too clever by half.
I had you tutored, but I could not teach you.
Your father was never a god
— such a bee in your bonnet —
he was just a man
though I could never make you believe it.

I knew more about bees, superfamily *Apoidea,*
than he did.
Honey-drudged through the mildewed tomes
while he played long-distance father
for thirty minutes a day
to you and your baby brother.
And why for him all the credit?
Ich weiss nicht was soll es bedeuten

He never acknowledged my work
I drafted his lectures, marked his quizzes
(as, I demur, you played secretary typist
for your husband, *Ach,* a woman's work is never done)
called me mere copy editor of his life
me with the work-weary black-carbon fingers
the burgeoning brain, the knowing for him.
Scantiness:
a breakfast paper smile here
a cup of tea there
razor-burn dry kisses
only teaspoons of gratitude

but I accepted it all with good grace
Anything for you and your brother
Attended your graduation on a stretcher
I only wanted the best for you
Surely, that is not too much to ask?

He was not a just man, just a man.
I pity us both for that.
More's the pity.

The Father Speaks

You were such a pretty little thing
bright as a honey-bee
doing its *ceratina dupla* dance
my sweetmeat daughter

Sivvy: Tense

It's present here
Present perfect
    I have gone
Present progressive
    You are going
Present perfect progressive
    You have been going
I struggle with the simple present
    I am I am I am
Present Subjunctive
    I looked as though I were dead
Progressive means continuous action
    You are going to come
and I remind myself
that Present can indicate Future

Without a schedule
I am nerve-frayed
I remember what you said
Write poetry after the oatmeal
Read one hour of Shakespeare
Spend some time on languages
before lunch
you and your conjugations

To develop a timetable is difficult!
One hour of counting the pale wraiths
trickling through the portals?
One hour of mimicking their Panic-bird cries?
One hour of writing letters
when I correspond with only you
black hole, your letter slot a coffin?
One hour of being coxswain for Charon?

Time, the river Scamander
It seethes, is ceaseless

I will myself into the future
Shall = simple futurity/mere expectation
 I shall be delighted to meet with you tomorrow
I hope the statement is not contrary to fact
 You will be coming
 You will be coming

The Daughter Speaks

I loved you
though I never really knew you
my fingers feel Kodachromed
from tracing your face
in photographs

I flex them
over my page
over my canvas
to give you back
your gift

The Son Speaks

Migration of the salmonid
the histological model
home-stream interaction
habitat culture

They really want to return
to their place of birth
They really want their mothers

Mommy!

riverriverriverriverriver

Sivvy: First Meeting

I loved you before I met you
my daemon, my platonic other
(If I were being facile
I'd say kindred spirit)

I loved your words
the solipsism of your jaguar
I could be there
when the hawk rose from your roost
to match the cunning swoops
in your sky

I knew you would be tall
but you took my breath away
soaring upward like the balloon of my heart

I wanted to touch that
hank of hair
falling
falling
and tuck it behind your ear
(Bathetic, clichéd, I know)

As if you knew
you robbed me of my hair-band
without constraint
for you
I loosened
myself an arrow
I loosed

Sivvy's Tribunal Speaks

You were always an "A" student
but here you have much to achieve

You were in some doubt about
your treatment before
Let there be no such doubt here

You must realize that the cure
is within yourself

You must overcome past fears

You must learn compassion
for yourself and others

You must cease dependency
and gain intimacy

You must learn to accept uncertainty
as the only certainty

You must learn to love yourself
You must learn to love yourself

The Tribunal has spoken
It is now up to you

You have all the time in this world

Sivvy: on Teaching

I was never one
to suffer fools gladly
Here's another teacher at the chalkboard
outlining the rules for Purgatory
determining the treatments

He nods thoughtfully
at our questions
He leaps closer to us
to show his passion for instruction
penetrating as a mosquito
irritating as a gnat
He enervates
He siphons my energy
I could dissect him

We were good teachers, weren't we?
Some of my students called me brilliant
Some of yours called you something else
but we will not think about this
We were right to give it up

He bores me
I rewrite the stanza on paper scraps
What I wouldn't give for some good bond
letter quality
Poesy still my chosen god
though She and you have deserted me

Everyone drowses
but the teacher and me
He backs off, titters
I mirror him
The buzzing energy misguided
the stick insect legs
I skewer him with my eyes
He gyrates, panics

Let him be the object lesson
until you get here

Sivvy: Harry Potter

I could have been a Rowling
you left me a single mother after all
I had the mind for fantasy
in my far-flying beds
and the realism too
Max and his yellow suit
If only I'd had more time!

I was able to predict my own death
even able to bring it about
no need for a Trelawney
in her mock poet gowns and capes
without a Ouija board, faux psychic

I too speak Parsel tongue
It came from years
of living with you
the forked tongue
the shedding skins
even now, sibilant intonations
whispered in my mind's eye

a landscape of beasts
more monstrous than Hagrid's
those vanquished with simple spells
mine shape shifting
in my infernal eternal landscape

The scar on my cheek
(Remember when I bit you on yours?
I wanted you marked as my *Doppelgänger*)
a belated re-birthmark at nineteen
My scar throbs with a foreboding
deeper, darker than Harry's
It pulsates exquisite pain
more of late
Can I hope that you are near
Can I hope that you are coming
you whose name, Lord, I may never speak?

Sivvy: Bait

so I'm lithe as a fish
You should know
You always dealt better with those
without language
with the cold-blooded
reptilian tails heartbeating on the dock

You liked to do your own bloodletting
The knife slice clean as a scalpel
Your excisions neat
They healed easily
if one were not already

dead

The Blighted Biographer Speaks

I couldn't say
what I wanted to say
It was as if a daemon
guided my hand
She importuned me
She wearied me
I did not ask for that disquieting muse
I did not want her

The Sister-in-Law Speaks

I never thought you
the sister I'd never had
A brother was good enough for me

You were provincial, colonial
Which cutlery
or hand
to use for your eating, gluttonous

Your French atrocious
Pig Latin for all I knew
No facility for languages

Your sad little poems
pinging like pebbles
against my brother

Intractable in your stony silence
Your basilisk glare
could jettison me
into mad rage
though not my brother

Whose hatred was colder?

That childhood game when you have to freeze
in whatever position you were in?
Since that February day
You have made ice statues of us all

Sivvy: Bowdlerising

so many years after my death
in *Birthday Letters*
you, husband, write of my journal pages
too little too late
but another ten
before the world opened them
fingers probing

Do I thank you for the Pulitzer?
1981 before you collected
my severed bits
the bits you severed
and reassembled them
mannequin of a willful smiling woman

You have meted out my fame slowly
though I left you my private papers
wrapped with fruity Christmas bows
glittering
under the yew tree just for you

Without you
I would have languished in a drawer
mothballed or moth-eaten

I am grateful
I am grudging
I am furious

literary executor
or executioner
the noose cunning and bejeweled
the unwary will step in it
a snare

Gratitude is metallic
and knocks against my teeth
An eye for an eye
a tooth for a tooth?
I shredded your Shakespeare
so you mislaid my late journals?
"lost" my *Double Exposure?*

I saw you and that harlot
reading and eating half pages
turnabout
bongo drums and poetic communion
How she grimaced as she chewed
I became part of her
she could not take
My paper was difficult to digest
How you backed up on my words
and how I roared with laughter

Journals neutered of my lust
The lulling ellipses
I expected it of Mother and the Letters
her prurience —
"If you haven't anything nice
to say, don't say anything at all" —
but not of you
Nothing of my voracious sexual appetite
Let's call it lust
Let's call it fucking
I fucked that Canadian boy hours after I met you
I'm a fire-swallower after all
even for you? especially for you?

Omissions and ellipses
for what I did to sweet Hamish
and, ah, Giovanni
Am I making you jealous?

but mostly those four dots
are about you
our whole lives in the spacings
my body open for you to ransack

How I loved your words
and thought you loved mine
All of my phrases about our conflagrant sex
One might think you flattered?

Through those omissions
sins of commission
I am being raped
you have raped me
and I long dead

posthumous
necrophiliac
you

Sivvy: Sleep

What I wanted was
not the gas
but sleep
dear sleep, kind sleep
a mantle, a tent
the dark shroud of my heart
my own home

Here I finally have enough
if I can blank out
Charon's constant gibbering
the shrieks of the souls in torment

I unravel the sweet sleep of care
between my other demands
and it knits up almost seamlessly

I am on my back half of the day
I never see the sun's rising, its setting
It's all a myth anyhow
as the world turns, and well, without me

You should know

And the seam becomes a bumpy hillock
like a welt girdling my body
a tumulus, myself cocooned

Sleep is not to be appeased,
wants more and still more of me and mine
With her fetid breath
she sucks in whole my days
my black dreams of you
my moribund drafts

And when I awake
and you aren't there
with whisker kisses, mugs of coffee
it is as if from the dead

My chrysalis a hard hard thing
the silk has become calcified
a specimen jar, glassy
and out of it will come
no butterfly
not even a dazed, glazed bee
or me

Sivvy: Climate Control

I thought it would be hot
here in Purgatory
like our honeymoon in Spain
Instead the wind rattles my bones
I look like a staccato speaker
but no words, no pearls fall
from the blue lips of this mute

My curse to have every day a Monday
and to be cold, so cold

now, here,
but especially in your England then

in Whitsun House in Cambridge
the gas fire a demanding beast
that chomped down my shillings
but I was grateful
my hair drying
luxuriant in the gaslight
the long shadows good company

and in 55 Eltisley
you and I had to pay extra
for gas and coal
but I told Mummy
"We'll keep the place extravagantly warm!"
and we did

Do you remember?

but it was harder at Court Green
in Devon, those cavernous rooms
I painted red for the illusion of heat
almost colder inside than out
the food never spoiled
even when left out on Assia's dining table

I had the deep freezer of home
but I wanted its central heating
the Grand Canyon's hot red heart

Those space heaters I lugged
from room to room, crimson or not
it didn't matter
myself a supplicant
worshipping closer and closer to those
punishing taunting little gods

A rash of chilblains over my body
House a frost box
And without you, in London
that chilly flat
its wide white floors like snow
so frozen solid
I could not leave any tracks, any prints
no matter how hard I tried
no matter how hard I cried

and I was cold, so cold

lonely

warm, so warm
the gaslight my only
friend

The Victorian Novelist Speaks

I imagined giving love
dying for love
my Heathcliff elemental
as of the sky, as of the earth
You did it
You had *your* Heathcliff
You might have been a kindred spirit

That day
in the crotch of my tree
you sat, imagining me
I shook its branches around you
A sign
An omen
Wuthering

Sivvy: Posture

They lined us up down here
like criminals
mug shots
front, my nose bulbous
and then not my best side

like those ridiculous posture pictures
at Smith
I never look good in photographs
even fashion spreads, too static
My animation is through life

I remembered to breathe deeply
to pull my shoulders back
to be proud of my height
a marionette string from my hips
through my head

What is my crime?
I hadn't planned for success
I wanted sweet rescue

I've been given a number
not yet tattooed on my forearm
but branded for my
heartreasoning love of you

Sivvy: Agenda

Why am I here?
It's like those days at Smith
The meeting room foetid
with teacher costumes, chalk dust, ennui
Pale yawns passed
with the grainy circulars
a slow motion drill
without grace, beauty
Sagging choreography
Sapping strength
You remember me then

Now, all is subterfuge, subtext
the whispering tribunal
the soft whiz of bullets
fusillades
not on target

Why are we discussing this
across dimensions of time and space?
Purgatory is punishing enough
without the meetings

Sivvy: Thesaurus

When bone idle
I flip through mine
an old friend
It no longer speaks to me

inclination   yearning   idolatry
flame   devotion
to lose one's heart

abhorrence   loathing   umbrage
pique   dudgeon   spleen
repugnance   odium   aversion
detestation   antipathy
estrangement

you love child
the words are not right

I am sore sick of my thesaurus
It does no good down here
the paper almost thin enough
to see through, not reflective

I need something that you can see
that will have you running
as you did not
that night

The book fragile kindling
I will strike a light
great black clouds
of carbon harder than diamond
smoke signals from Styx
of words gone rotten

The Late Night Talk Show Host Speaks

Oh yeah, so you're
with me on that one

whadya think?
a drum roll?

and isn't she
the one who stuck her head in an oven
and wrote about the ovens

sorta an ad for Easy-Off, eh?

I guess she got a lot of flak
Hehheh — get it? — flak
about it

Did you hear there's a McDonald's near Dachau?
Say, over six million served

The Holocaust Survivor Speaks

Death snowbreathed my wizened cheek
How restful to be
inhaled by him
dark cajoler
but I did not
I did not

You were not there
You cannot know
A ghost of the truth
your pale pale pain

You do not do
You are not *du*

Sivvy: Abortion

Q. What's black and white and red all over?

I believe in life
I believe in choice
of course, language should say
what it means
especially in
the poetry of the body

suction like the deflating of a balloon
a scrap of red
a party favor gone dead
dilation and curettage
that purposeful scrape

having had it done
three times
(as many times as my suicide attempts),
your mistress said made it an art

It is no art

but better that crimson canvas
those painterly, systematized strokes
than your having had a child with her

when I heard
I rained with clotted blood tears
I became a heaving statue

and she used my suicide
she and the child both

and now they use *my* images
fetal death as genocide
thumbprint eyes all knowing

how dare they appropriate
the silent screams
of gelid Auschwitz Jews?

Remember the real victim

Sivvy: Colour I

You think I saw only in black and white
pen and ink
my life and brain bipolar
the rods and cones of sheepdogs' eyes

my market drawings of Benidorm
Emily's ruined croft
beached boats off my beautiful Nauset
only rubble, flat relics

but it was you who
wore black
saw black
were black

you forget my smudged pastels
my cheerful pots of paint
but I remember the seashell of daffodils
the opal light off our children's faces

you never liked me in blue
and my hairband
it was not blue
but red

Man in black,
You lacked my red
You forbore my red
You seduced my red
so I gave it you, to you
viscous as menstrual pulp

Don't pretend you never wanted any of it

your world was leached of my colour
Your world in black and white
a flat photograph unchanging
Like Crow, you have become
blacker than ever

Read my red red lips
Smell my crimson lipstick

You need my red healing solution
my Mercurochrome love
It stings but only for a minute
and it heals sweeter than
honey

Sivvy: Political Correctness

Do not paint over our murals
and pretend it never happened
History is all plum, "herstory" too
Easy to use this language
harder to use it well
to enjoy it

So my *Bell Jar* Esther saw herself
as smudgy-eyed Chinese
looked like a sick Indian
was as yellow as a China man
kicked a Negro — just desserts?

So Tar Baby arrived with the Bee Box?
Don't like those "African hands"
No matter it's a peculiar species of bee?

Have me do it all again?
Forget the appellation "Lady"
before "Lazarus" because
biblical characters should be gender free?
Eliminate "black" from my work?
Have Esther accept Joan's advances?
Tell her she likes her?
Provide her with the pleasure
of the tongue, of the text?

With this talk
I am gagging
I am sore bored and bothered
I am white heterosexual woman
Wish to edit me out?

I love what my tongue can do
I loved your tongue
but what of other tongues?
any race, any sex,
the bleached blonde Negress?
I am lonely down here
and you are taking so long

I long, I long for . . .
Sexual allegiance takes no prisoners

The Freudian Critic Speaks

I may be no academic
but I know the terms
penis envy
Electra Complex
goddess

bitch

Sivvy: Furlough in a Computer Store I

To: http:\\youknowwho.exe

From: you know whom

Subject: greetings

so curious the lightness of my fingers on the keys without
the heft of a typewriter without the snap of the cartridge as
it barreled back it seems too innocuous to be an implement
of destruction mummy as always wrong, she so keen on
my typing for a big strong businessman for my learning
shorthand for a big strong businessman and those pothooks
I hated I could never learn them and why and what for
everyone is his own secretary now though I suppose I would
still be sending your manuscripts through cyberspace to
publishers you did not know existed or maybe I could be
your secret infection worming into the chambered nautilus of
your heart and you said you hated the *telephone,* you arrogant
bastard try all the function keys now delete delete drive C
colon slash delete YOUR HARD DRIVE IS DESTROYED

Sivvy: Furlough in a Computer Store II

To: http:\\youknowwho.com

From: you know whom

Subject: ☺ emoticons ☹

after what u did 2 me

what combination of
parentheses and colon
semicolon and asterisks
could convey my hurt
my blistering rage?

;-/ skeptical?
;-> sarcastic?
:~/ mixed up?
:-& tongue-tied?

I shall have to invent
a new lexicon
a Sylvia symbology

Sivvy: Furlough in London Drugs

Blood pressure monitor constricts
arm in a vice
no flow to my writing hand
Panic bird overhead, fluorescent

They've given me the man drug
for mothers giving birth
The pain contains sweet forget

But it frees me
How bright and light
A whole aisle of portable heaters
Coleman stoves
The largesse

I recognize Vitamin C
but what of these others?
St. John's Wort, Echinacea
Germanic gutturals
black black

Pharmacists in white coats
sibilant secretive language
Naproxen Zoloft Prozac
measured, measuring
their treasure sacks
panacea, but I want it all

your love was my placebo

Sivvy: Without Feathers

In your black turtleneck
a uniform for an edgy soldier in peacetime
or the skin of a new animal
one you wouldn't hunt out of whimsy, caprice

you test your snares with
big fingers, ham hands, hooks
and they come up bloody
dripping with poems

my poems
yours?
ours

The Mythologizer Speaks

You have become
your own White Goddess
riding abreast of the Moon
You are your own eclipse

Sivvy: Review

Extra cash is always handy
You know I'll write anything for Mammon
Perhaps a new pseudonym?
Victoria is done to death

A new soul turns out
The BC Health Guide
He is not you
He looks ghost-pale, ravished
The book better in theory than in practice

I leaf through the tome
such smiley faces
they make me uneasy

Maybe I had PMT
not enough leafy greens
or SAD
the drizzly mist
of your Devon autumn that stretched to spring
the next and the next
now without you
still without me

I broach "Anger and Hostility"
"Try to understand the real
reason why you are so angry"
I offered the best years of my life to you
a mere man, like my mother before me, despised
my world as much a soap-bubble planet as hers
It is too real here

"Draw or paint to release the anger
or write about it in a journal"
My journal
which contracted my anger to a crucible
which you destroyed

"Forgive and forget"
Such object lessons
If only your harlot were not on the level
below

"Home Treatment" for "Anxiety"
"Then say to yourself
'Okay, I see the problem
Now I'll start to deal with it'"
You, it's always been you
even when it failed to resemble you

Under "Sleep Disorders"
"Don't take sleeping pills
They can cause confusion
memory loss
and dizziness"
or take a lot
Time in a bottle

"Plant a plant or pet a pet"
Poison ivy
hawthorn
jaguars
snakes with forked tongues

"Stop all negative self-talk"
Perhaps Thalidomide, a vitamin pill now

"Send yourself a steady stream of affirmations"
Such mawkish prose
More stilted than mine ever was

I look up "Home Treatment"
and "Suicide"
I did it at home
twice
even if I failed
in that cellar

I did use my "common sense"
as the book advises me to do
"Do you feel there is no other way?"
"Do you have a suicide plan?"

"How and When do you plan to do it?"
Why, this is a suicide's manual!
Shall I claw the cover with my hot talons?
Shall I give it my blood-stamp of approval?

But they forgot about the rusks and the milk
What to do with two motherless children
yours

Is the publisher's area code 9-1-1?
May I edit the second edition?
Is it already too late?

Sivvy: List

I could see you
as in a glass darkly
The cave wall was cold and chilled
Where it ended and I began
I couldn't tell

Others, just thwarting stalagmites, cold obstacles

I may have been boy-crazy
even as a child
Jimmy with his roller-skates
I had the key
John with his duplicating machine
and pretty messages of love
Ilo, *Ach Ach,* and our talks about art
He startled me

The frisson of pleasure and morbidity with Emile
but he meant nothing to me
Dick and Perry with their insufferable mother
perhaps even worse than mine
Hard to be in love with brothers

Gordon only so smart
effeminate with his Joyce quotes
and poetry without your heft
Peter the same
he with his Bostonian
fading smile approaching, self-aggrandizer

Phil John Bob Myron Lou Gary Art
I'm running out of fingers here!
Eddie a life-line, though better
to have been without flesh
All those little men on the crossing
I forget their names, it is not important
below the water line most of the time

even in Cambridge
Iko, Mallory, David
with his stories of ice and chilblains
through him I met you
intermediary Bert
I never slept with him
but he sold me your first words
the pimp of poesy

even Sassoon, sweet Richard
sickly Richard, exotic Richard
not for me in Paris
Not for me to be
an arm chair
for a lap-sitter
a Santa to his dour child

Only you were big enough for me
your bear arms would wrap around me
Only you heard the steady drip
of the stalactites
and in them
we could laugh at our funhouse reflection

Sivvy: Bills

your strumpet dismayed
by my gas bill?
tried to get my friend to pay?
a false economy
a tin heart

at least no bills here
only purgatory, not penury
though there are always wants
the long distance charges
would be telling
if you would stay on the line

I would dial person to person
have my own operator standing by
and a Value Added Tax

my room and board paid in full
pallid putrid buffets
of mostly potatoes
but my own room
no Mummy
no you

priceless
without measure

Sivvy: Panic, My Alcatraz

Heart
a trapped bird
a fusillade of fibrillation
not even the Bird Doctor
of Alcatraz could tame
me, a caged animal
The first sign
But there are more

Up there
it was teaching classes
a strangely fetal poem
your absence, always your absence

Here, panic floods my body
My blood is antifreeze
I am halfway across Lethe's bridge
and am sure I will die
I have to keep walking
I want to meet you, I must meet you
though I am already underwater
with no equipment except faulty lungs
Each is envelope thin
There is no air

My body removes itself
from my brain

"The cold tide its wall"
makes my peninsula
an island
Does the bedrock beneath really join?
Which to what and how?
"The island itself was the prison."

Most prisoners of Alcatraz
stayed eight to ten years
I am here for life
There is an hour
in a minute
The bridge's stanchions wobble like rubber
Injured bird
I keen as I try to move forward

The reading will keep me sane
I must read, this I must do
"The months pencilled on the wall
with the days scratched off."
I could gouge out the minutes, the seconds
in the bridge's concrete
with my little claws
but I cannot get out of my body
that moves limpet slow

Even "Al Capone's cell,
five by nine feet,"
is larger than mine
I occupy all the
solitary
confinement
cells simultaneously

Heraclitus said you can't step
in the same river twice
but I do, I do

I am my own jailer
Jailer and prisoner both
Steel bones, concrete brain
Intricate girders
The prisoners confined in Alcatraz
were the ones who built it

My nerves crackle their own
"electrical locking mechanisms"
My sliding cell door
is even now being bolted shut
My power is even now being
extinguished
My screams are Munch silent

"Ma Barker's son Doc
was killed trying to
escape
(They told him to come back up,
and he said he would rather be shot,
and he was.)" Laconic.
Would that it were so simple

I want to meet you, greet you
without leaving
my island

Sivvy: Furlough in Brueghel

If this is to be an object lesson
I should have chosen
Landscape with the Fall of Icarus
my best sea closing over
the scissoring legs
or *The Blue Cloak*
with its colours of folly
shades of vice

not *The Triumph of Death*
Red, red, so much red
I'd thought you the lute player
me holding the songbook
and you
lyrics of love the tie that binds

but you have proven yourself hyena
or red skeletal horse of war
from the book of *Revelation*
and I am all the skulls
all the garroted corpses
the simulacrum of the fire
the burnt tree with its limbs
pleading for any heaven

Sivvy: Furlough in Las Vegas

for Scott

The paper work was torture enough
In triplicate is not poetry
I had asked for illumination
I wanted the sea's brightness, its light
I tried for Truro, Wellfleet, even Providence
but I've passed over whole states
a rushed déjà vu of our cross-country tour
now on the outskirts of Death Valley
closer closer

No potato people here
nor you
all sequined star fruits
No cow life
all a glitter
too bright for my eyes
be careful what you wish for
Mummy always said

Rainy days in Devon
uniform grayness
closing in

I wished for Ocean 1212-W
not these fake beaches of Mandalay Bay
a dim reflection of my beautiful Nauset
no waves to sigh on the pure shores
palm trees on the skyline, not right
the sea should be open

Malevolence in the slot machines
lechery in the buffets
the very air gluttonous
Swords thrust hourly in Excalibur
Arthur an old vague myth
of someone who may or may not have been
a Merlin

I hover like a bumblebee

An Elvis marries a couple
she not in a pink wool suit
he not in standard black
Witnesses in feathers and tassels
After, they all dance
in blue suede shoes
My bare toes tap out the rhythm
The Elvis has a forelock like yours
but less oily

Hotel rooms opulent
Oh! the bed!
a life raft
Six pillows
a softness to love hugely in
but you are not here

Bathroom bigger
than our entire flat
at Chalcott Square
This tub without the back-up sewage
of my last lonely winter
without you

The names here I could use in poems
Bell aj ee oh
Mandalay so liquid, so resonant
Bell Man
these words I enjoy
The syllables fall off my tongue

It's worse than a barnyard
worse than Purgatory
with Charon's balefulness
high voices in the elevators
Atlantis sinks
Roman statues, colossal, talk
Giant cats in aquariums stalk

Acrobats! trapeze artists!
and I have only to step
in the middle of them
to cause the traffic
to shriek to a halt
I'm sure I still have it in me

But nobody stops
I am shouldered in the throng
somewhere a volcano explodes
every fifteen minutes
Where is my fame?
Where are you?
I need you to translate
to explain the rules

I find a quarter
left in a slot
The video poker machine
calls like Ouija
a full house
our delightful children
her, you, me
an odd threesome
She would do better here than I
with her harlot's clothes
her gaming table smile
The plated nickel falls through my fingers

I must get my bearings
not think about her
The Paris is not like anything I have ever seen
painted cumulus in the robin sky
an aborted leg of a papier-mâché Tour d'Eiffel
Will I meet my Richard one third life-size?
How small he will be!
not like you
never like you

Memories waft
Gypsies
Tarot packs

Sad eyes on the tables
Different names
baccarat and blackjack
I always recognize black
tables for high rollers

I motion a sleek waitress
for a drink
She ignores me
Women never liked me
much

Here the high stakes of life and death
Three watch me with baleful eyes
I'm a sleek cat they cannot cage
Not neurotic
like that freakish creature, albino,
of Siegfried and Roy
(faux men, not like you)
excreting in the pool

The shows! How affected!
How puerile!
I can climb higher than five storeys
I am five stories, ten novels,
one hundred, a thousand poems
whole and beating, heartthrobbing

But even *here* are Germans
the long hallway of the Mirage
a Polish Corridor
I can't get away from them
And here another Elvis! and another!
I will not play any spurious Sylvias
I am the real thing!

I waft by the Coke store
The figurative has become literal
My mind swims in tropes

I cannot see my moon
amidst all the light
neon, ersatz sun

I am still dark
It does not help to be here
You are not here
My currency no good here

Where am I?
I want to go home

I click my heels three times
and nothing
Why am I wearing blue suede shoes?

The Betrayer Speaks

Grasses in envelopes
pebbles, stones
caves moors
He loved them
and me
Nothing would have worked with you

Hisssss

Sivvy: Furlough in Klee

I believed in
The Triumph of Wit Over Suffering
You expected me to become
the splayed anorexic *Virgin in a Tree*
limbs gnarled as old boughs
dugs like dogs

True, you made me lose my appetite
your desertion soured me
but my old lusts will never be lost

I repel sea-monsters in the *Seafarer*
balanced in my coracle
I have found my sea legs
I can do what I like to you

You have become the sniffing dog
in *Woman and Beast*
scenting me out

I can escape in Klee's lines
a twittering quirk
the delicate pastels
the violent violets
I would like to be
a mosaic of shape and colour
a *Demon-Lady*

but we are forever etched
Klee's *Mask of Fear* on four legs
we are as knotted
as an *Oath of Ghosts*
dead-ends and cul-de-sacs
a ball of Mobius strips

where you stop and I begin
I cannot begin
to know

Sivvy: Furlough in the Periodic Table

I asked for my beautiful Nauset
the blue H_2O
ready in my bikini
despite a post-pregnancy belly
face mask, snorkel, flippers

Where is the sea on/under which to swim
The air is sulphurous
stink bombs and hissing test tubes
I see through wavery glass
as loopy as a bell jar
I am out of my element
whichever one it is

In this periodic table
it's more cramped than in Daddy's ear
I move across the irregular board
in little flipper hops
Cu Ag Au copper silver gold a lustrous chain
but far from hydrogen and helium
atomic

Chemistry almost destroyed
my life
once
I cannot let it again

Gas comes from *Chaos*
Boyle's law, Charles' law
it makes no nevermind
What the volume pressure temperature
If you touch me
I will explode

You think you're a law unto yourself

Intermolecular forces of attraction
oil and water
plutonium and americium
we cannot mix

I want to move
the stasis is killing
I must become kinetic theory

Joule Kelvin Avogadro Gay-Lussac
Let the laws become my mantra
van der Waals
incantatory words
to beckon and beseech
Somewhere chalk scratches on a blackboard
like iron nails

I struggle to take off my face mask
for a better look
but it's welded on
And it's you I see at the front
of the lecture hall
You are the Laboratory Master
of all you survey
You juggle a Bunsen burner
a crucible a bolt of fire
You handle the elements

You write on the board
in your slanty print
So this is how we will communicate
across the abyss

What does that mean? *Was bedeutet das?*

Problem to solve: worth 100%
show all calculations
before you leave

The blood of deep-sea divers
becomes saturated with N^2 and O^2

                                  of the air that we breathe

under the

                                  poem safety in poetry

comparatively high pressures
characteristic of the depths

                                  so slimy but I forgave

at which divers work.
If the pressure is relieved
too rapidly (e.g., too rapid
an ascent to the surface),

                                  (Let me return)

the N^2 comes out of the solution rapidly
                  Oh, God, this is so removed from poetry
and forms bubbles in the circulatory system
of the afflicted divers.

                                  I am sore afflicted
                            and I need rescue and tools.

This condition, known as the "bends,"
may be fatal.

                                  May may may may I
                            dwell in possibility.

One solution to this problem

                                (Please, let me return,
                        I will be forever in your debt.)

involves the use of an artificial
atmosphere of He and O^2 in place of air.
                         You are the very air that I breathe.
(He is not very soluble in blood).

                                Letting and Spilling.
                    I am no longer hot for your blood
                              please believe me.

Oh, God, I'm drowning, not waving,
help me, I am not crying wolf,

If the helium-oxygen gas mixture

will you still love me?
If you do not touch me
I will explode

Sivvy: Colour II

Many said
Better dead than Red
Political vitriol
Ecstatic polemics

I always preferred
your Fascist love
I always enjoyed
the sense of Red

The Benefactress Speaks

Watching my ant farm,
I awaited news of you
even from your Mother

For you, anything
tuition, fees for McLean
the best mental institution
birthday cheques
money for a wardrobe
a new barrette
pretty in your fiery hair

You sent me snippets
often secondhand
I longed for more

I loved you
and your husband
I was not wrong in that

I congratulated you on everything
teaching news, publications, reviews
your move to Devon
housewarming
heartwarming

You made me so proud
but I told you, be careful
Please turn down the heat,
only glow

But you were always
incandescent
conflagration
burnt offering

You poor soul
You never could read me
though I believed us kin

Almost-daughter, I didn't want
only
a
dedication

Sivvy: Court Green

if one could become a place
I would Court Green
the land   mine
all   mine
or ours

the round dining table
storing it for . . . her
storing it beneath our place settings, our stews

your attic study beneath the eaves
the best front bedroom for mine
Indian rug on the little one's floor

my sewing table
the playroom bay window
red corduroy curtains

We should have had a school of children

the cobbled stone hall
the wine cellar filled with jams
ancient sink, gas stove

Love made our house

beyond our windows
the stinging nettles, the apples
thorns on blackberries
the elm, the yew
church steeple
shallow step into the garden
our daughter's hand warm in mine

then pattycake on the grass
another finger game
open the door and
here's all the people
crowing

hours
in the garden
dandelions, lilacs
the sheaves of daffodils
the fallacy of the seasons:
Easter harvest

our little girl eclipsing the sun
with her arms full of yellow

and best
our crimson bedroom
the heart's shivered core

The Other Famous Suicidal Poet Speaks

Having planned the longer
I am the stronger
Just remember who
thought of it
of everything
first

Sivvy: Furlough in the Pop Culture of the New Millennium

I)

Who is this Madonna?
She has more hair than my bald ones
more breasts, more voice too
Though furred and blonde
she's not a Marilyn
and I wouldn't trust her with
emery board and orange stick
She is fearful as a Munich Mannequin

and yet she has children!
a girl and a boy
even as I had, as we had

Their fathers bred bastards
One of them you?

II)

What is this reality TV?
What is this Survivor idiocy?

The Tribal Council has spoken
I have the talking stick

I vote you all off the island
Yes, you, too, especially you

It is my island
I am the island

III)

The Ladies Home Journal
looks the same
"Can this marriage be saved?"

Can it?

Sivvy: Furlough in the Modern Classroom

These Creative Writing students
speak to me
even less
than my students at Smith
those long years ago

another command appearance
— exasperating! —
My stool is wobbly
My wave is feebler than the Queen's

Today they snicker
behind lank hair
      but can't a poem mean
      whatever you want?
They discount that De Chirico's painting
and my poem bear the same name,
ignore such marked clues
but wish for more
      but can't it mean?
      but who says so?
      wow, margaret laurence and sylvia plath
      on the same day!
Sullen sarcasm has replaced measured irony
but they must be poets
because they abhor punctuation and grammar
use the lower case for names

I can see her, Margaret,
unlovely wraith
no longer even handsome
in the far corner of the classroom
Sad nun fingering the rosary
of her fingernails
as the students
yawn over the copies, passing passing of
The Diviners, The Stone Angel

I would like to talk to her
about her decision to quicken the end
about writing that promotes pain unto death

She keeps to herself
back home
She who had a coterie of young writers
while on earth
her cottage, her body
their home

not for these students
chewers of cud
measured burps from each of their four stomachs
no heart, no soul
but always something to ruminate over
cellulose and chlorophyll
for self-reflection

They don't hear me or Margaret
who gazes at her cramped hands
as if for guidance
Their eyes are focused
on the middle distance

Even the Queen is allowed to go home
to put her feet on the coffee table
to thumb through a fashion magazine
a shot of brandy in her tea

Margaret is fading at the futility of it all
and I, shortly
We could be in a barn
for the hot animal stink

This is worse than Purgatory

The Friend Speaks

Manic when I pencilled
in your margins
my notes
you were never any friend of mind
I mean, of mine

Sivvy: Coffee

When not appropriating mine
you favor
domestic images
Here's another

All my men were
tea to your coffee
a thin brew, herbal
palliative, all floridity
Marlowe's meadows to your
rock-bound Raleigh winter
Even now, even here
literary allusions just roll off my tongue
You appreciate them

You, rich espresso
Panic bird eyeing the brown liquid
its murky depths
into which I could swim
My hands would settle
around the milky mug
you made for me
I drank deeply
I was wired, I was hooked
I wanted more and still more
numbness

I sleepwalked through our days
sick from caffeine
falling down fetal, oh to sleep, to sleep
nursemaid me with a conduit of pure caffeine
give me more of your sweet poison

Sivvy: Man's Best Friend

(and woman's also?)

you never were much for dogs
though you used them in your youth
sniffing, hunting

too earth-tethered for you
all stunned obedience
undeserved loyalty
love-lit eyes
leashed, fawning

you preferred foxes wolves bats
circling birds of prey
those not feckless but cunning

now in *Birthday Letters*
you say you were
dog, protective, loyal
stalwart by my panicky side

I am barely paraphrasing
weary weary
dog-tired

Were you a dog?

Through our dog-eared days
of dog-eat-dog writing
when I found every day
doglegs against which I ran smack
until I could hear the cry of hounds

even then
were you the dog's kin?
not *canis familiaris*
plush friend with the lolling tongue

but *lupus,* predatory wolf

The Former Pen-Pal Speaks

I didn't have a short man's complex
I gave you good advice
and love

You should have listened to me
You should have married me

I understood you as no other
superficial, snobbish, yes
but like no other

Sivvy: Furlough in Rousseau

I pipe the snakes
everything phallic, voyeuristic
warping undulations of the lake
leaves, petalled heads

I weave an Eden
the pink of the stalking bird, labial
My breasts, orbs of moon
My pubic hair, serpentine
all silk liquid, especial

even without you

Sivvy: Second Furlough in Rousseau

I look along my arm
beyond the end of my finger
tip
pointing
luxuriant in my black hair
luxuriant on my red couch
breasts an extra set of eyes
big
I enjoy my nakedness
I belong here
in *The Dream*

Beyond the end of my finger
beyond the startled animals
the feathery boas
the floral plumes
my green boudoir
at my command
I imagine you arriving
barely beyond my frame of reference
like a pointillist dot
slowly coming into focus

Sivvy: Furlough in the Lilly Library

Each box a small coffin
Her[e] is my dismembered body
bony relics
ashy sheaves of me
brittle leaves of me
Communion
I am the host

Let the proffered wine
be your blood

The Post-Structuralist
Literary Theorist Speaks

roses collapse
into petals and thorns
the occasional worm

all that is certain
is that it is uncertain

one might say
in a fantastical world
about textual entities
slipping into snares
gagging on the gorse

truth is as truth does

Sivvy: Phoenix

Last time
I left a note
gone for a walk, don't worry
Few walks last three days
Even Christ didn't drag
his cross that long
What was I thinking?
Cryptic in a crypt
Fierce purgative
Three days later
I vomited my way to life

This time, nothing survives me
except my two fat-faced children
yours too
I'd wanted something different
No pills
Just the gas
like my Mummy's lullabies
sleepy sibilant soporific

I thought you would come back
You liked my blue sparkly dress
In your eyes
I could see me reflected

I thought you would rescue me
my black black knight
even if mussed from another bed
I wanted to see myself in you

Three days again
from our Friday date to Monday
The neighbour off to early work
The au pair girl to arrive
and you, surely you

My timing razor dreadful
In those last moments
I willed you to come
My longing rising with the gas
Dawning sorrow, too
I never was good at physics
especially the physics of the heart

Sivvy: Furlough in Lorelei

My hand will not loose its grasp
not unfist, not unfurl
What's this?
A mirror from a lady's dressing set
curlicues of Trojan bows
and arrows, the mane of a giant horse

My feet won't do as I tell them
What's this? From my hips
a silvery tail blooms and shines
I can see myself, many of my selves
ghostly in it
beached
closed

In my other hand
a comb, mottled pewter
heavy with longing
I comb my hair
root to tip
root to tip
long strokes
and pile it gleaming
on my head

I avoid my tail, the mirror
Mirrors have been against me
all my long life
Why should it be any different here?
My larynx throbs, my sinuses are clogged,
I must look a harridan

A rock dislodges in my throat
a gleaming, pretty pebble
projectile in the mouth of the river
As it roars into the reluctant ocean
the waves fall back hissing

I am alone on this island
of scrub brush, of runes and red rock
A crow alights and pulls on carrion
It flies away, entrails like a kite string

I have all the time in the world
I uncoil my hair
I will sing for you
It is a song Mummy taught me
It is a song she sang for me, lulling
long long ago

Ich weiss nicht was soll es bedeuten
Das ich so traurig bin

Do not worry, my dear one
Whatever the crew
I will guide your ship
into my safe full-throated harbour

Sivvy: Eye, Tooth

No one knows but you and me
and I have been gone for forty years
you for five
together, more the age of our daughter
An eye for an eye

What did you do in all those years
other than raise my children?
Rough justice. *Ach*
My plangent son, my reflective daughter
but I will not think on them

Assia? but I will not speak of her
vengeful strumpet
her name the hiss of rising gas
who tried to steal them away
even my death
a tooth for a tooth

you

and not of her, either
she with even less imagination
that former nurse

Did they say they loved you?
What did they do to prove it?
What could you have seen in them?

At least I was
always a smiling woman
I smile still, it is habit

What now?
Would you like more chitchat with the cocktails?
Molotov? *Ach, du*

My arms are tired from rowing
in exchange for stories, words
gobbets from Charon's toothless mouth
trembling, shining as entrails
in the prow his fluttering hands like a mute's
whispering the tarot of crossings, of descents
but these are not our Cambridge days
for God's sake, boating on the sleepy Cam
It's a stinking slog
but I will not think on that

and the other company is whiny and pale
They do go on and on
about the road not taken (bathetic!)
and loved ones left behind

Even so, every time a new
one swims through the fog
his face a bloated light
I start like a guilty thing
quiver

You

I have bloodied my knees, my palms
in looking but Daddy's not here
as you thought
Ach, du

Only me, *ich, ich*
travelling, waiting
my red hair flying
in my own special circle
loosening or tightening
like a noose
There is too much freedom
or too little

And why don't you come?
And why aren't you here?

It's been thirty-five years and then five
five long years
a seeming eternity

and I grow smooth and small
as a stone
the pebble on
a dead woman's third eye

The Husband Speaks

I have nothing more to say
Far be it
from me
to have the

last

word

Chronology of the Lives of Sylvia Plath and Ted Hughes

Not exhaustive, this chronology is designed as an aid in following the implied narrative of the poems.

1930 Ted Hughes is born in Britain.

1932 Sylvia Plath is born in the USA.

1940 SP's father, Otto Plath, dies, and her mother, Aurelia Schoeber Plath, supports the family.

1950 SP attends Smith College on scholarship, partially funded by a benefactress, Olive Higgins Prouty. SP dates widely over her college years.

1951 TH begins a degree in English Literature at Pembroke College, Cambridge.

1953 SP has a summer internship at *Mademoiselle* in New York. Later that summer, back home, she attempts suicide and is institutionalized for several months. Financial help comes from her benefactress. SP recovers.

1955 SP graduates from Smith College in English Literature.

1955–1956 SP attends Cambridge University on a Fulbright Scholarship. SP and TH meet at a literary party. SP goes to France on her own, hoping to meet boyfriend Richard, but to no avail.

1956 Secret marriage of SP and TH. SP's mother is the only family member who attends from either side. The couple has a six-week honeymoon in Spain. SP finishes her degree at Cambridge while TH teaches at a boys' school. His interest in astrology increases. They visit TH's family. Both love the Yorkshire moors, where the Brontës lived and wrote. SP and TH's sister meet.

1957 In America, SP teaches at Smith College while TH writes and publishes *Hawk in the Rain*.

1958 TH teaches for one term at the University of Massachusetts.

1958–1959 During a year in Boston, both write. SP has a part-time clerical job. She completes the story "Johnny Panic and the Bible of Dreams." She undergoes analysis with Ruth Beuscher.

1959 They travel cross-country in the States. SP is pregnant with their first child, their daughter Frieda.

1960 They return to Britain, leasing a flat at Chalcott Square. Daughter Frieda Rebecca is born. Publication of SP's *The Colossus* and TH's *Lupercal* in Britain.

1961 SP has a miscarriage and then an appendectomy. Plath and Hughes buy a house, Court Green, in North Tawton (Devon). They rent their London flat to the Wevills, a Canadian poet and his wife, Assia. TH and SP share time for writing and childcare at Court Green. TH publishes *Meet My Folks!*

1962 Birth of Nicholas Farrar. Visit to Court Green by the Wevills, in May. TH begins an affair with Assia in June. A summer of estrangement between SP and TH follows. TH moves out. In the late fall, SP and the two children move to London, a few houses from the former flat, in a house when Yeats once lived. *The Colossus* is published in the States.

1963 Worst winter London has seen in years. Under a pseudonym, SP publishes in Britain *The Bell Jar,* a novel based, in part, on her own experiences in 1953–4. The main character is Esther Greenwood. Plath commits suicide by gas in February. TH becomes SP's literary executor.

1965 Publication of SP's *Ariel* in Britain. Assia gives birth to a daughter, Shura.

1966 Publication of *Ariel* in the States.

1969 Assia gasses herself and Shura.

1970 TH publishes *Crow.* TH marries Carol Orchard. He divides his time between Devon and London.

1971 *The Bell Jar* is published in North America under SP's own name. SP's *Winter Trees* and *Crossing the Water* are published in Britain and shortly thereafter in the States.

1975 Aurelia Schoeber Plath publishes *Letters Home,* in which Plath frequently signs herself "Sivvy."

1976 Publication of SP's *The Bed Book* for children, written in the fifties.

1977 SP's *Johnny Panic and the Bible of Dreams: Short Stories, Prose, and Diary Excerpts* is published.

1981 Publication of *Collected Poems of Sylvia Plath,* edited and with a foreword by TH.

1982 *Collected Poems* wins the Pulitzer Prize. TH publishes *The Journals of Sylvia Plath,* which includes part of her work: the last journals she wrote were lost or destroyed by him, he admits.

1984 TH becomes Britain's Poet Laureate.

1996 Publication of SP's *The It-Doesn't-Matter-Suit,* for children, written in the fifties.

1998 TH publishes *Birthday Letters,* which wins many prizes. TH dies in October.

2000 Publication of *The Unabridged Journals of Sylvia Plath.*

2001 Publication of SP's *Collected Children's Stories,* including "Mrs. Cherry's Kitchen," previously unpublished.